Inversion

AF624481

Sheridan Powell

BookLeaf Publishing

Presentation by *BookLeaf Publishing*

Web: www.bookleafpub.com

E-mail: info@bookleafpub.com

ISBN: 9789395950480

First edition 2022

I dedicate this curated collection of musings to all the amazing women in my life. I am inspired by each of you.

ACKNOWLEDGEMENT

Many thanks to those who have encouraged me on this journey and provided warm words of support and love.

PREFACE

All too often we define ourselves in relation to those around us, who slip in and out of our daily lives. We define our worth by arbitary and ever changing measurements and our worthiness of love by the same token.

We find ourselves trapped between the three faces we display to the world and find the lines blurred between our true self and our outward presentation.

In writing this collection of poetry, I aim to explore different facets of my own identity and in acknowledging their compartmentalisation return the pieces of myself to a whole.

Unmatched

3am phone calls
Stolen kisses
Sparkling eyes

Unequivocal love

Carefree adventures
Flirtatious texts
Post work naps

Unmistakable love

Midnight flights
Lazy Sundays
Milestone celebrations

Undeniable love

Missed calls
Empty seats
Lost opportunities

Diminishing love

Fading memories
Unspoken words
Unfamiliar voices

Dying love

Words unspoken

I rehearse the sounds in my head
Rolls the vowels across my tongue
Titillate my mouth with reverberations
Clean the saliva from my teeth
Clear my voice for words I will never speak

I count the syllables that dance in my mind
I reformulate the sentence
I rephrase and restructure
Is it better to stay silent?
I retract from the words I will never speak

I write heartfelt phrases and pull them apart
I doodle love hearts and flowers
I emphasise your name and place it next to mine
I almost dare to say it out loud
Silently, I mouth the words I will never speak

The consonants of our names dance in my throat
The sibilance hisses up my spine
Broken promises sit on my lips
Heartfelt sentiments lie dormant in my heart
I swallow the words I will never speak

Dreamless sleep

The pillow beside me lies empty
Devoid of your form
I long for your shape
I'm lost, my heart torn.

The space where you lay
Indented with your soul
Lies vacant in waiting
To make my heart whole

The bed that we shared
Made for two not one
Is too large by far
Now that we're done

I sleep a dreamless sleep
No more nooks or cradles
To place my heart inside
This lost love without a label

3am in December

The birds cry for daybreak
I cry in mourning
For what was lost, never to be found
No new awakening, no dawning.

Instead there is just darkness
In the empty space that remains
No voice escapes my lips
But salty streaks do glisten my cheeks

The world is in eclipse

And I, here in the midst, do sit
And wait…
My soul abates, yearning for the morning sun
A chance to start anew.
Fresh
(if only that were true)
Here I lie blue
My final thoughts of you.

Possibilities

I loved who I thought you were
I loved who you led me to believe you could be
I loved the idea of you and me
I loved the notion of we

You had no intention of making it so
No desire to nurture our love to grow
Blow after blow

As the future crumbles, I lie in the remnants of
false hope
Unable to let go

Searching

I search in your soul for a trace of me,
Listening for my heartbeat.
Does it not lie there?
I reach out for your love but clutch thin air.

Would you love me better if my smile lit up a
room?
Would it make your love bloom?

Would you love me better if my body was out of
this world?
Would you claim me as your girl?

Would you love me better if by cosmic design
you gazed into my eyes and our stars did align?

Would you love me better if my laugh was
melodious and sweet?
Would it make you want to keep me?

I search in your eyes and hope it's all lies
But the vacant gaze does little to hide the fading
light
Of a love that is lost

Still I wonder and hope in this now familiar
trope
Will I ever be a star in your galaxy?
Or am I a ball of dust, waiting to combust,
devoid of your lust.
Waiting to be just
Enough.

Worthless

You don't look at me with love and affection,
but still I wait under the pretension, that you will
give me all your attention.
Unreservedly, committedly, undivided-
provided, I am worthy.

A caveat.

You don't deserve me!
I cry, you shout, on more than one occasion, but
by whose equation?
How did you tally up the score?
Show me the calculation that proved I was
valued less and you were worth more.

Show me the figures.
I will work it out. My mind spins and whirls.
Pop!
That seed of doubt.

It buds and blooms signalling impending doom.
Upon spiteful words and cruel jibes it feeds like
a leech, growing in each, sowing discontent, hell
bent on approving your measurement.

A scale by which no one can compare.
My soul laid bare.

Let's settle this score.
I am worth more.

Fractured

Broken, fragmented, shattered.
I need glue to be fixed.
Not glue, you; but you left.
Left me bereft.

How now can I be fixed?
Kintsugi? No, I am not worth gold.
My soul has been sold, given to another to hold,
to help us grow old.

Discarded.

Tossed. Cast adrift. No time to fix.

No care to try. Broken I lie.

Affection

In your arms I lie and you cradle me
A space in your body is made for me
Your lips graze my neck and pull me tight
I will never be the same

Rejection

Your words are barbed
Filled with poison and malice
Venom spills from your lips and penetrates my veins
I will never be the same.

Salvation

The cord between us is tired and frayed
Yet you remain at the edge of our universe
Soul tied, bond broken, trust lost.
We will never be the same.

Loss

A thin red line.
A black screen.
A blue uniform.
A cool white tile.
A silver tap.
A cornflower gown.
A small pink pill.
A crimson thread.

Home

I slide into the vacant seat, still warm from the heat of another soul
Their plump body had wandered off, to continue its journey.

Home?

Home. What a subjective little noun.
A house is not a home. You have to make it so, make it homely.
Adjective. Imbue it with trinkets and memories trapped in silver frames
Then maybe you will achieve a sense of homeliness.

Pour velvet cushions into it, wrap it in woollen blankets, flood it with woven rugs, bathe it with candlelight.
Fill the rooms with the voices of little people.

In a shell of my design I live alone.
A house is not a home.

Hysteria

A wandering uterus.
Yours, mine, ours.

Individual diagnosis, collective possession.
Uniquely feminine.

A mad woman in the attic, consigned to her fate.
A woman trapped in the wall paper, to sit and to wait.
A woman locked in a cage, without a voice.
A woman enshrined in a portrait without a choice.

We're all mad here.

The space between her legs

Fetishized, the space between her legs is
objectified.
Lust swirls just at the thought of it.

Objectified, the space between her legs is
viewed by the male gaze
She shrinks in its vision, intimidated by opinion.

Star gazing, the space between her legs is a
world of wonder
Yet to be explored by a wanton adventurer.

Wondering, the space between her legs is
fortified
Until men decide she is worthy of its promise.

Fortification, the space between her legs a
physical barrier; preventing intrusion
A tantalising challenge, a protected virtue.

Intrusive, the space between her legs is
medicalised
Prodded and poked she lies prostrate.

Medicalisation, the space between her legs is up for debate
Her body, her choice is my mandate.

The space between her legs is hers and hers alone.

The space between my legs is mine to own.

Objectification

Madonna or whore, which do you desire more?
A binary of two extremes.

Shall I play the devout or would you call me out.
Frigid.
Shall I be the flirt or would you treat me like
dirt.
Tease.

Should I be an accomplice to your unsolicited
words.
Good sport.

Should I reject your advances and take my
chances.
Bitch.

Which version of womanhood would you like to
see?
Devise the definition, place in a category.

Objectify me by your polarity
Half of humanity.

We do not fit neatly into your box
You'll see.

Almost motherhood

We sit on the brink of almost motherhood
Single, childless, alone.

We are crushed under the weight of paternalistic expectation
Of turning a house into a home.

We are caught between worlds, cultures, identities
A biological instinct we must bear.

We are encumbered with an internal clock
Endlessly ticking with despair.

We take action! Step by step intervention.
Prodded, jabbed, frozen.

We shoulder blame, condescension and pity
Some hearts truly broken.

We are entitled geriatric long before our time
Put out to pasture before our prime
Step up to the production line
Quick! Before your eggs decline.

I step back from the brink of almost motherhood
And contemplate my womb
I am divinely feminine with or without
I am not yours to commodify or consume.

Kindness

Pour your glass half full
Throw the scales away
Slice yourself the juiciest peach
You made it here today.

Light your favourite candle
Devour that bestselling book
Plan that trip you longed for
It's your hard work, not luck.

Belt out that anthem
Unbutton those jeans
Speak kind words to others
Follow your dreams .

Be the light in your own life
Put yourself first
Take care of your needs
Let go of the hurt.

Love yourself a little harder
Forgive your mistakes
Open a new page
The world is yours to create.

Past

Let go my dearest love, you have held on too long.
I know you are strong but it's okay to be weak
To seek, to want, to desire more
to be unsure.
Let go of before.

Present

Keep going my dearest love, your work is not done yet.
Move past this regret and open your heart.
Be brave, be daring, be great!
Make your own fate.
Don't stop yet.

Future

Hello my dearest love, you made it here.
A day you thought you would never see.
Smiling faces, warm hands, little feet.
Hit pause, play, repeat.
You are happy.

www.ingramcontent.com/pod-product-compliance
Lightning Source LLC
Chambersburg PA
CBHW051754130826
49812CB00033B/1146
9789395950480